Narcissism

Transcend Gaslighting And Manipulation, Conquer
Anxiety And Depression, Reclaim Your Agency,
And Attain Mastery Over Your Life

*(Anticipate The Unforeseen By Gaining Insight Into The
Motivations Behind Sociopathic Behavior)*

Sheldon Frenette

TABLE OF CONTENT

What Is Narcissism?... 1

Can Narcissists Love? 33

On Traveling Anonymous 47

Dialectical Behavior Therapy...66

Mitigating The Effects Of Gaslighting From A Disparaging Acquaintance 78

Etiology, Clinical Manifestations, And Consequences 85

Coping With Vindictive Behavior 118

Observing Narcissistic Behavior..................................129

What Is Narcissism?

The term narcissism, referred to as Narcissistic Personality Disorder (NPD) in professional discourse, is frequently employed in our society that is fixated on self-portraits and fixated on famous individuals, usually to designate an individual who appears excessively self-centered or egoistic. From a psychological standpoint, it can be argued that narcissism does not encompass genuine self-affection. It is a more rational assertion to state that individuals diagnosed with narcissistic personality disorder (NPD) harbor profound affection towards an idealized and magnified perception of their own selves. They hold an affinity for this exaggerated self-perception, as it conveniently shields them from profound feelings of vulnerability.

However, sustaining their inflated sense of importance entails substantial effort—and it is precisely at this point that the maladaptive mindsets and conduct become relevant. Narcissistic personality disorder encompasses a consistent display of egocentric, haughty cognition and behavior, a dearth of empathy and concern for others, and an all-consuming desire for adulation. Individuals with NPD are frequently perceived by others as exhibiting traits such as arrogance, manipulation, egocentrism, pretentiousness, and a propensity for making demands. This cognitive and behavioral pattern permeates every aspect of the narcissist's existence, extending from professional engagements and social connections to familial relationships and romantic attachments.

Individuals diagnosed with narcissistic personality disorder tend to exhibit a pronounced reluctance to make adjustments to their behavior, even in instances where such behavior is resulting in negative consequences for them. Their inclination lies in shifting the burden of responsibility onto others. Furthermore, they exhibit a high level of sensitivity and respond excessively to even the most minor criticisms, conflicts, or perceived slights, perceiving them as personal affronts and reacting harshly. For individuals who are involved with the narcissist, it is often more convenient to comply with their requests in order to mitigate their aloofness and outbursts. Nevertheless, through a comprehensive examination of narcissistic personality disorder, one can acquire the ability to discern individuals exhibiting narcissistic traits, safeguard oneself against their manipulative tactics, and establish appropriate limits for personal well-being.

The Misconceptions About NPD:

The majority of individuals will exhibit at least one narcissistic trait during the course of their lives. These behaviors or mindsets could be characterized as narcissistic, but they distinguish themselves from a diagnosed personality disorder due to variations in intensity, frequency, and duration. There exists a variety of personal characteristics, exemplified by attributes such as generosity and discretion. They are evident in varying degrees in every individual. The aforementioned phenomenon occurs with individuals possessing a narcissistic disposition. Narcissism, or to some extent, certain characteristics associated with it, may be present as a personality trait in certain individuals. In some individuals, the extent and profound nature of these narcissistic inclinations are so severe that it perpetually hinders and causes harm to their interpersonal interactions and self-perception. Narcissistic tendencies as a personality trait may, on occasion, manifest themselves in certain facets of our conduct or convictions.

For instance, it is possible that you have a persistent antagonistic relationship with a colleague. This may incite you to engage in sarcastic remarks in their presence or distort the expression of admiration you convey.
obtained from your superior during their presence. Perhaps you might even choose to provide them with an exceedingly unfavorable critique at some juncture. However, this response is

sporadic and limited to a specific individual, rather than being a pervasive disposition towards all others consistently. Conversely, narcissism remains a enduring and characteristic trait in individuals diagnosed with Narcissistic Personality Disorder (NPD).

To illustrate, an ongoing rivalry exists between yourself and all colleagues, including your superior. Based on your conviction of possessing superior intellect and aptitude compared to them, it follows that you should assume a position of greater authority and responsibility. This occurrence took place during your previous two employments. On the whole, you perceive yourself as significantly more esteemed than the individuals you encounter in educational, occupational, and other settings.

It is important to bear in mind that NPD qualifies as a psychological disorder. It does not pertain to any individual or entity.

-exhibiting social confidence
-being ambitious
-taking great pride in their authentic achievements
-having great self-esteem
-maintaining their physical appearance -attending to their physical appearance -ensuring their physical appearance is well-maintained -acknowledging the importance of physical appearance and taking measures to uphold it -devoting efforts towards maintaining their physical appearance -putting emphasis on the upkeep of their physical appearance
-being keen
-disliking you e.t.c

Reasons for NPD

The development of narcissistic personality disorder may be influenced by environmental factors, including cultural and upbringing influences. individual goals and success) compared to collectivist cultures (which prioritize the needs and goals of the group over the individual)." "According to certain studies, there is evidence to indicate a positive correlation between narcissism scores and individualistic cultures, wherein greater emphasis is placed on individual aspirations and achievements, as opposed to collectivist cultures that prioritize the collective needs and goals over individual ones."

In individualistic societies, emphasis is placed on the rights and ambitions of each individual, while in collectivistic cultures, the collective good of the community takes precedence.

In the aforementioned study, scholars conducted a comparative analysis of narcissistic attributes between individuals raised in former West Germany, which epitomized an individualistic society, and those raised in former East Germany, known for its inclination towards a collectivistic culture.

The results indicated that individuals who were raised in West Germany exhibited higher levels of narcissism and lower levels of self-esteem when compared to those from East Germany. Furthermore, scholarly investigations indicate that aside from cultural factors, early life experiences may be a pivotal factor in the development of Narcissistic Personality Disorder (NPD). Adverse childhood encounters, such as parental rejection or disciplinary actions, can potentially contribute to the development of Narcissistic Personality Disorder during one's adult years. Simultaneously, an excessive amount of parental commendation can contribute to the development of Narcissistic Personality Disorder (NPD).

Existing research indicates a correlation between diverse approaches to parenting and the presence of narcissistic characteristics in adult offspring. However, it is important to note that no singular parenting approach invariably results in the development of narcissistic traits. Alternatively, the confluence of parenting methodologies and other pertinent factors such as genetic predisposition might interplay to manifest NPD.

Typically, these parenting attributes are associated with a gradual ascent in narcissistic tendencies among children: excessively vigilant or overbearing parenting, insufficient displays of affection resulting in limited structure or limits, commendation exclusively focused on excellence or unattainable expectations, mistreatment, or acts of maltreatment. One investigation suggested

The association between excessive parental vigilance and the presence of both sensitive and grandiose narcissistic traits has been observed in young individuals. Furthermore, an excess of admiration was linked to an inclination towards grandiosity, whereas insufficient restrictions were found to be associated with a vulnerability to narcissistic tendencies.

Genetic Factors: It is plausible that genetic influences may contribute to the development of narcissistic personality disorder. According to a study carried out in 2014 that examined 304 sets of twins, it was found that certain characteristics associated with Narcissistic Personality Disorder (NPD) exhibited a significant degree of heritability. Specifically, the trait of grandiosity was determined to have a heritability rate of 23%, while entitlement showed a heritability rate of 35%. Nevertheless, these traits were observed to be distinct from each other.

Prior research suggests that Narcissistic Personality Disorder (NPD) exhibits a higher degree of heritability compared to other personality disorders falling under cluster B. Personality traits could also potentially influence the manifestation of NPD. Grandiose narcissism is commonly associated with characteristics such as a sense of entitlement and a brazen emphasis on oneself, alongside overbearing or dominating behavior. Conversely, vulnerable narcissism is defined by traits like introversion but a strong preoccupation with oneself, coupled with high levels of neuroticism (moodiness) and an oscillation between feelings of immense pride and intense shame.

Types of Narcissism

There exist three fundamental categories in which narcissistic behavior can be classified. The three categories may possess similar characteristics, however, they originate from disparate upbringings.

Furthermore, these three categories establish the diverse behavioral patterns that individuals will exhibit within interpersonal connections. They are:

Grandiose Narcissism:

Individuals exhibiting this behavior were commonly regarded as possessing a sense of superiority or elevated status during their early developmental stages. These expectations may continue to influence them as they transition into adulthood. They have a tendency to engage in self-aggrandizement and exhibit an attitude of haughtiness. Individuals who possess grandiose narcissism exhibit tendencies towards aggression, dominance, and an inclination to inflate their own significance. They possess immense self-assurance and display a lack of sensitivity.

Vulnerable Narcissism

This behavior often arises as a consequence of neglect or abuse experienced during childhood. Individuals exhibiting this behavior demonstrate a remarkable degree of sensitivity. Narcissistic behavior serves as a means of shielding oneself from feelings of insufficiency. Despite their fluctuation between feelings of inferiority and superiority towards others, they experience a sense of disquietude or offense when others fail to acknowledge their exceptional qualities.

Malignant narcissism

Grandiose narcissism has a more pronounced association with malignant narcissism compared to vulnerable narcissism. An individual displaying malignant narcissism may manifest numerous characteristic attributes of narcissism, including a pronounced inclination for admiration and the pursuit of being elevated above others. Furthermore, malignant narcissism can manifest as: malevolence, deviance, deriving pleasure from the suffering of others. Additionally, individuals with malignant narcissism may exhibit certain indications of antisocial personality disorder. This suggests that individuals with malignant narcissism may exhibit an increased susceptibility to encountering legal complications or developing substance use disorders.

The initial instruction is to engage in contemplation.
This term is of significant magnitude! It pertains to a process of contemplating profoundly and meticulously, examining an object with keen and deliberate attention.

Wherever one directs their attention, their focus will inevitably be drawn. It is impossible for it to be otherwise.

Harboring an intense preoccupation with the notion that something is amiss regarding an individual in your vicinity will compel you to diligently acquaint yourself with every pertinent detail pertaining to the matter. What may not be readily apparent to you is that it ultimately guides you towards your personal objective. Furthermore, not solely for the betterment of your own well-being, but rather for the preservation of Life itself, which is compelled to manifest in great abundance through your being. In this manner, consequently realizing your individual fate.

Please transcribe this term onto a sheet of paper and position it in a location that will allow for regular visibility.

Deliberate and contemplate upon it with thoroughness and diligence.

The act of introspection requires patience and a willingness to attentively heed your inner musings, rather than rushing through the process. Now is the opportune moment to meticulously strategize a course of action to regain control of your life from the oppressor. From the individual whose underlying motive is to exercise authority, influence, and exploit you for personal gain. Their plans do not encompass any provisions for your involvement. If they provide you with alternate information, they are merely engaging in deceptive promises for the future.

The advantages that you bestow upon them are ultimately futile, squandering your precious time, physical and mental energy, and the entirety of your existence. This endeavor proves to be ineffectual due to the narcissist's inherent incapacity to exhibit gratitude or contentment.

It is imperative, therefore, to reflect upon one's life, its significance, and its intended objectives. Have you derived any insights from the experience of being subject to their circumstances?

Develop a sense of self-importance and acknowledge your intrinsic value. Engage in contemplation and exercise diligent and deliberate thinking.

You have persevered through all of these experiences; what significance do they hold? Is it possible that your presence on this planet during this period has been intended to assist those who are likewise compelled to endure the challenges of this daunting journey? Perhaps you are present to elicit their authentic essence of existence. Is your intention to aid them in discovering their inner divinity from a non-theological standpoint? It will become evident in due course that the influence of God is minimal or non-existent in matters of organized religion, while it holds utmost importance in relation to yourself.

The biblical narrative surrounding Job recounts his initial loss of all possessions and subsequent restoration to a state of abundant prosperity prior to the culmination of his life. He experienced an increase in progeny, affluence, and opulence beyond what he had possessed prior to this.

Engage in thoughtful reflection upon this particular statement: "Remain calm and acknowledge that I, the Almighty, am present," and proceed to repeat it to yourself several times, attentively absorbing the message it imparts. Remain calm and acknowledge that I, GOD, exist! The profound realization of the authentic connotation behind this statement may instill a sense of fear within you.

What does this mean? What implications might this carry?

You will gradually come to recognize that the narcissist is not entirely unfounded in perceiving themselves as a deity. However, before delving into a detailed explanation, let us further elucidate the matter. Our society places significant emphasis on individual personality. Our identity and our potential can be effectively encapsulated within the realm of professional trajectories or enterprising endeavors.

According to the guidelines, it is incumbent upon us to exert diligent effort towards attaining success, cultivating intellectual prowess, and achieving prosperity, among other aspirations. Our system is founded on this fundamental concept, which, while not incorrect in its adherence to a particular framework, begs the question: is this overarching principle entirely accurate?

Reflect upon, engage in thorough and deliberate introspection, and you will perceive within yourself the embodiment of success, fulfillment, intellect, prosperity, and even wealth. It is regrettable that the majority will fail to comprehend this, as we have misapprehended its true nature all this time. There exist an abundance of diversions deliberately crafted to instill feelings of inadequacy, helplessness, insufficiency in terms of appearance, and a yearning to possess characteristics that lie beyond our own selves.

You are among the select individuals designated to uncover genuine self-awareness in this environment.

Apologies! I appear to have unintentionally offended an individual of strong religious convictions, who recognizes and expresses the presence of a divine force within myself. Unbeknownst to individuals, an internal aspect assimilates within them, ultimately shaping their identity and personhood.

Remain calm and acknowledge that I exist as the divine being. If you are indeed a divine being or, at the very least, a representation of divinity, then all that is required of you is to maintain a state of tranquility. Then affirm within yourself, "I am inclined to do so."

By engaging in this action, regaining control of your life from a self-centered malevolent deity becomes remarkably effortless, causing you to admire your inner resilience. This power is intertwined with the Origin of Existence, and although it belongs to you, it is not exclusively yours. All HE requires of you is to acknowledge the presence of I within you. That I AM GOD!

Please be aware that you are not being requested to relinquish your existence, nor are you being mandated to align with a religious belief system or any similar entity. It is within your knowledge to identify yourself, simply attune your attention to your inner reflections in a state of tranquility.

The ruling leader acknowledges their divine status, and you express discontent towards them for this! Why do you harbor frustration when it is you who lacks self-awareness? This is the reason for which he exerts control, manipulation, and mistreatment over you.

The perception of the narcissist holds some truth, although it is only partially accurate, as he solely recognizes his own divinity while neglecting the fact that we are all manifestations of the Divine.

You will grapple with this truth, and even if you were inclined to perceive yourself as such, how could others possibly do so, particularly those of such malevolence?

This is the perspective from which our personality perceives it. Our ego perceives this situation in a similar vein to how a narcissist perceives themselves as the only being deserving of the divinity. In our sense of self-importance, we have an inherent desire to exalt ourselves at the expense of excluding the divine.

Despite the potential negative impact on our personal prosperity and financial success, we must prioritize acknowledging His absolute authority and embracing His intended path for us, instead of solely pursuing our individual ambitions and desires. The two are intertwined.

It seems that you have chosen to endure extreme hardship and cling to your independence from Him, even at the risk of your own demise, rather than embracing the concept of Him residing within you and experiencing a life of abundance and contentment.

The individual afflicted with Narcissistic Personality Disorder is fully aware of your identity and is determined to go to extreme lengths to prevent you from uncovering the truth. If one lacks self-awareness, they are susceptible to becoming malleable and accommodating to the desires of others, potentially even assuming a subordinate role to a narcissistic individual as they assert control over their dominion.

The narcissist exists devoid of a soul; it has been dispossessed from within them. We have an insufficient understanding of the method, and it is not a matter of significance. He harbors no affection, instead coveting your own and employing every effort to pilfer and assimilate it, in order to appropriate your love and virtues for himself.

He has only experienced a semblance of love in fleeting moments of physical intimacy. It is ephemeral and must swiftly recede, engendering within him a sense of vacuity, disgrace, and impotence once more. He seeks a reservoir of affection, and on every occasion he believes to have discovered the individual who can provide it, love eludes him. Despite his inability to discover it or control it within himself, his intent is to annihilate your own.

You reside within me just as I dwell within you. God manifests his presence in the physical realm via his creations, by means of you and me, with utmost significance on our part. All beings shall ultimately bear witness to the marvels of the Almighty, including even individuals of dissenting nature, such as the naysayer.

Did he not, in the end, by virtue of his malevolence and ferocity, guide you to the utmost depths of veracity with regards to the nature of God and your own being? Now, you can embark upon a truly fulfilling existence, and ultimately, akin to Job, the subsequent phase of your life will be truly extraordinary, encompassing a multitude of blessings, including but not limited to material wealth on this earthly realm.

Regardless of what you may aspire to, whether it be the act of creation, the pursuit of a fulfilling existence, or the experience of love, these desires reside within you and manifest through the very essence of your character. Acquire a deep understanding of the objective aspect of your being, comprising of Love, Wisdom, and Power. Through achieving a state of stillness, harness your breath to pacify your mental activity, attentively listen, and you will experience favorable outcomes.

You are about to acquire strategies for regulating your thoughts and managing your cognition. These strategies will have a profound impact on your life when implemented effectively. This demonstrates the method by which individuals triumph over those who have embraced Narcissistic Personality Disorder (NPD).

If you are able to master the regulation and guidance of your mental faculties and divert them towards your intended destination, the experience will be akin to being thrust into a pugilistic arena with a person who exhibits narcissistic traits.

The audience erupts with thunderous applause and marvels at your prowess, skillfully executing juggling, aiming, and striking actions. Each round ends with a decisive victory, while the individual in question, displaying a lack of courage, meekly retreats to a distant corner of the ring, grappling with disbelief over what transpires. You will have the privilege of claiming the title, securing an indisputable victory. Now is the opportune moment to contemplate your aspirations in life, record them in writing, and collectively embark upon the journey of realization.

I can surmise that one of your aims is to experience a sense of well-being on a daily basis. Achieve this by envisioning the person you aspire to be. Consider a person whom you hold in high regard.

I initiated my personal voyage by stating: "

I am a manifestation of the divine will, intricately crafted by a higher power. I possess qualities that are highly sought after, and I am a competent and innovative professional in the realm of business.

Allow me to elucidate the fundamental essence of this assertion; being a sacred manifestation crafted by the divine signifies that I possess unique intentions and talents which ought to be disseminated amongst society, and no individual displaying narcissistic tendencies shall impede my progress.

To possess desirability entails directing my attention away from perceived imperfections, such as scars, and instead emphasizing my prominent features, like my well-proportioned, elongated legs, along with other appealing characteristics. If you direct your attention towards your shortcomings, that is precisely what others will perceive.

Lastly, as a seasoned professional with a dynamic entrepreneurial spirit, I acknowledge and embrace exceptional leadership attributes within my own persona. In the past, there was a propensity to direct my attention towards the adverse emotions residing within me. I am committed to dedicating ample time to methodically construct an influential empire that harmonizes with my personal vision.

Upon realizing that all internal self-dialogue embodies affirmation, one will attain clarity in recognizing the superior value of cultivating positive affirmations until one's thoughts manifest into reality.

Engaging in positive self-affirmation and consistently undertaking small actions each day will facilitate personal growth and catalyze the transformation into an enhanced iteration of oneself.

Can Narcissists Love?

Each individual who has experienced the presence of a narcissist inevitably ponders, 'Does he genuinely harbor affection for me?' Does she hold my presence in high regard? Their emotions are in conflict, torn between affection and pain, hesitant to stay or depart, yet discernment eludes them. Certain individuals assert that they are the object of affection, whereas others hold steadfast in their conviction that they are devoid of love.

It is puzzling due to the fact that they may come across an affectionate individual whose companionship they enjoy, only to be subsequently faced with behavior that leaves them feeling inconsequential or inadequate. Do individuals with narcissistic traits exhibit genuine feelings of affection towards their families and partners?

An individual diagnosed with Narcissistic Personality Disorder (NPD) is typically unable to experience and express emotions of genuine affection and love as commonly understood by the majority of people. While it may appear unkind, numerous facets of Narcissistic Personality Disorder are incompatible with the concept of love. Narcissistic individuals might exhibit affection and engage in considerate behaviors, yet their expressions of love typically depend on the reciprocation of what you can provide for them in return. In many cases, individuals with Narcissistic Personality Disorder frequently engage in transactional interactions within their relationships.

Love does not exhibit qualities of self-centeredness, conceit, manipulation, or jealousy. An association with an individual who exhibits NPD, whether in a romantic or platonic setting, can prove to be detrimental, filled with turmoil, and in certain scenarios, profoundly destructive.

Due to the inherent absence of empathy in narcissistic individuals, they may encounter challenges in cultivating feelings of love towards another individual. This concept may prove challenging to apprehend, especially for individuals who possess strong affection or close ties to a narcissistic individual, such as a relative or companion. Nevertheless, it is imperative to acknowledge that narcissism exists on a spectrum, and certain individuals exhibiting narcissistic tendencies might demonstrate superior aptitude in demonstrating affection and reciprocating it. The challenge lies in determining their true identities, which could prove to be quite arduous. Gaining extensive knowledge about narcissistic personality disorder (NPD) will enable you to effectively engage with individuals who exhibit such traits.

Whilst the narcissist may engage in efforts to ameliorate their conduct, it is ultimately incumbent upon you to assume responsibility for your own actions and choices. You are not responsible for their emotional reactions, thoughts, or actions directed at you. Acquiring knowledge about the condition and equipping oneself with tactics for engaging with a narcissistic individual is a highly commendable course of action, particularly in instances where there is uncertainty regarding their capacity for both giving and receiving affection. If one possesses the awareness of their capacity to experience love towards others, it would be advisable to exercise prudence and employ certain measures when engaging in any kind of interpersonal association with an individual exhibiting narcissistic tendencies. It is advisable to adopt a well-prepared and educated approach.

An individual may be subject to gaslighting, excessive affection and manipulation.

It is imperative to establish and uphold suitable boundaries when involved in a relationship with an individual diagnosed with Narcissistic Personality Disorder (NPD). This constitutes a significant mental health issue, and it is imperative to promptly seek therapy.

HOW A NARCISSIST LOVES

During the initial phase of courtship, individuals with narcissistic tendencies may display strong feelings of ardor.

Nevertheless, this fervor is consistently directed towards their endeavors, ambitions, and creative visions. It entails self-love rather than love directed towards another individual.

These types of alliances elicit favorable recognition and contribute to the narcissist's sense of self-worth and psychological gratification in terms of their sexual experiences.

Interpersonal connections tend to possess transactional qualities in the case of the majority of individuals exhibiting narcissistic tendencies. Their objective is to derive unencumbered gratification. They are engaged in a competitive activity with the objective of achieving victory. They exhibit proactive and dynamic behavior, in addition to possessing a high level of emotional intelligence that enables them to acknowledge, articulate, understand, and regulate their emotions. This grants them the capacity to exert influence on others in order to garner their affection and admiration.

They derive satisfaction from being held in high regard, well-liked, and contented. Additionally, their exceptional interpersonal capabilities facilitate the establishment of a favorable initial perception. They could exhibit a strong inclination towards exploring romantic prospects and enticing potential partners through acts of generosity, professing love, employing flattery, engaging in intimate relations, fostering romantic connections, and making enduring promises of commitment. Certain individuals with narcissistic tendencies engage in dishonesty and/or employ excessive demonstrations of verbal, physical, and material expressions of fondness in order to manipulate their intended recipients.

Narcissists exhibit waning interest in circumstances where increased proximity is expected.
A significant proportion of individuals encounter challenges when it comes to sustaining a lasting relationship beyond the span of six months up to a few years. They prioritize power over relationships and view vulnerability as indicative of weakness. They avoid establishing connections in order to maintain control, displaying a preference for maintaining authority and asserting superiority over others. Therefore, engaging in game-playing achieves a desirable balance between satisfying their requirements and maintaining the freedom to interact

with multiple individuals for the purpose of romantic or sexual relationships.

Certain individuals with narcissistic tendencies tend to engage in relationships with a primary focus on their own goals and ambitions.
Additionally, there is a likelihood that they will cultivate favorable emotions towards their partner. Nevertheless, these sentiments are more inclined to be rooted in friendship and shared interests. Should they decide to enter into matrimony, their motivation to uphold their romantic charade would diminish and they would likely employ defensive measures to evade emotional closeness. When subjected to interrogation or faced with unfulfilled desires, their demeanor turns icy, their judgment sharpens, and their anger intensifies. They demonstrate a greater

propensity to align with the demands and desires of their spouse, especially when it aligns with their convenience and their sense of self-satisfaction. They should explore alternative sources of validation in order to compensate for the damage caused to their relationship due to their self-aggrandizement.

When individuals are sufficiently motivated, they may exhibit displays of affection.
Their affection is contingent upon the narcissist's response to it. Given the fact that narcissism encompasses a continuum of traits and behaviors, ranging from moderate manifestations to severe and malignant forms, it becomes increasingly apparent that in cases of severe narcissism, pronounced self-centeredness and the inability to display affection are heightened. Dating or engaging in long-distance

relationships that entail lower expectations tend to be less arduous.

Individuals exemplifying perfectionistic narcissism exhibit a disdain for others and may actively seek to eliminate adversaries in order to uphold their steadfast pursuit of perfection.
All these imperfections serve as impediments for narcissists in accurately perceiving the reality of another individual, encompassing their fondness towards them. Indeed, narcissists possess a level of emotional intelligence that enables them to cunningly manipulate and exploit individuals in order to attain their objectives. However, their deficient emotional empathy renders them insensitive to the detrimental consequences of their actions.

Narcissistic individuals occasionally exhibit traits of aloofness, indifference, or aggression, but they are not devoid of the capacity for benevolence and assistance.

Narcissists do possess the capacity to perceive and cognitively understand the emotions of another individual.

NOTE:

The challenge posed by genuine narcissists lies in their inherent inability to comprehend the detrimental impact of their behavior on others. Frequently, they demonstrate an inability to acknowledge their own narcissistic tendencies. If you confront them about it, they might become defensive instead of acknowledging their errors. It is crucial to bear in mind that a crucial element underpinning this condition is the pervasive belief that the affected individuals hold a position of superiority over others, characterized by enhanced intellectual faculties, exceptional competence, and overall superiority.

Their rationale may be based on the assumption that in the event a relationship is not functioning well or one is experiencing dissatisfaction in it, the sole responsibility lies with oneself. They may maintain that they are not responsible. Numerous individuals encounter difficulty in maintaining relationships with individuals who consistently refuse to apologize or acknowledge their mistakes.

Ultimately, if one is in connection with an individual possessing narcissistic traits, it is plausible that they might develop affection for them. Nevertheless, it is essential that they recognize their behaviors and make a conscientious effort to manage them. Establishing a successful relationship may prove challenging if one is involved with a narcissistic individual. Narcissistic Personality Disorder (NPD) is regarded as a manifestation of a personality disorder characterized by individuals who typically encounter difficulty in modifying their behavioral patterns. It is important to bear in mind that recalling this information could facilitate your comprehension of why they encounter difficulties in expressing empathy and love in distinct manners. Additionally, it could facilitate the act of pardoning the individual for any transgressions.

Asking whether a narcissist harbors feelings of love towards you is an ill-advised inquiry. While it can be beneficial to comprehend the psychology of such individuals, couples may inadvertently place excessive focus on the narcissist, potentially leading to negative consequences.

Contemplate the extent to which you are regarded with value, esteem, and compassion. Are your anticipations being fulfilled? If this is not the case, how does this influence your sense of self-worth, and what steps can be taken to address it?

On Traveling Anonymous

According to empirical research, the presence of companions and social connections has been found to enhance one's confidence, self-assurance, as well as foster a sense of inclusivity and an inherent sense of direction. One potential issue associated with rapidly forming friendships is our tendency to overlook signs of toxicity in our new acquaintances. If we were to do so, it would alleviate a substantial amount of tension and emotional distress.

Occasionally, we observe individuals with whom we are affiliated behaving contrary to their normal demeanor. In such instances, it is advisable to enhance one's powers of observation and remain vigilant in order to identify recurring patterns. In a formal tone, one could say: "Alternatively, it is advisable to engage in conversations and seek information from individuals who possess a more comprehensive understanding of them compared to your own." If you happen to be fortunate to receive candid disclosure, you can discreetly devise your course of action.

Toxic individuals frequently exhibit a sense of superiority and may presume that you possess a level of naivety that would allow them to maintain their charade; this presents an opportunity for you to gradually distance yourself from such associations.

According to the advice given by Paul in his initial correspondence to the Corinthians (15:33), it is crucial to remember that associating with unfavorable company can lead to the deterioration of one's virtuous nature. Therefore, in your endeavors to cultivate new friendships within a foreign setting, it would be prudent to gradually distance yourself from individuals who exhibit undesirable conduct. One could commence by gradually discontinuing the sharing of personal information pertaining to oneself, acquaintances, and relatives. If they persist, provide them with ambiguous responses or information.

Iyanla Vanzant imparted, during an interview on the Oprah Show, the wise advice of actively avoiding potentially harmful or chaotic situations by metaphorically crossing the street when one detects signs of instability or madness.[1] And she is entirely correct; if you start observing warning signs and actions that are incompatible with your own, my dear, swiftly traverse that road with all the swiftness your limbs can muster. Authentic fortitude lies in exhibiting the audacity to disengage from any trivial matters. One should refrain from abruptly discontinuing their consumption. In the event that you do, they shall become aware of your discernment of their manipulative tactics and shall proceed to devise new strategies.

Please keep in mind that maintaining an attitude of indifference is highly effective in safeguarding oneself against individuals who exhibit toxic and manipulative behaviors. However, in the event that you happen to resemble the individual I once was and are unintentionally provoked, it is conceivable that you may inadvertently bestow upon them the ability to exert additional emotional control over you. Once they determine the means by which they can exploit your vulnerabilities, they will commence crafting deceptive strategies to derive sustenance from your emotional reservoir.

Do not be misled by their excessively amiable demeanor. Toxic and manipulative individuals often present themselves as exceedingly benevolent and modest individuals when initiating any kind of relationship. In the realm of companionship, possessing traits of modesty and humility is highly commendable. However, it is worth noting that individuals of an egocentric and toxic nature often employ modesty as a facade, concealing their underlying arrogance. Exercise heightened caution as individuals may obscure their genuine personas from others for prolonged periods, spanning months or even years. However, in due course, their underlying belief in their innate superiority will inevitably become apparent.

In certain instances, such as the one I am currently facing, you may find yourself grappling with an individual who exhibits the traits commonly associated with a classic narcissistic personality. Now, let us proceed to delve into the clinical evaluation and attributes associated with individuals displaying narcissistic traits.

Who is a Narcissist?

A person exhibiting narcissistic tendencies often possesses an exaggerated perception of their own significance, a profound yearning for excessive recognition and praise, and tends to demonstrate a deficiency in empathy towards others. Individuals diagnosed with narcissistic personality disorder (NPD) exhibit clinical characteristics of self-absorption and an inflated sense of self. The following are several attributes that serve as indicators of an individual with Narcissistic Personality Disorder.

They exhibit a pronounced sense of entitlement and demand unwavering admiration on a regular and excessive basis.

Consistently seeks acknowledgement as being superior, even in the absence of any notable contribution that justifies such recognition.

They persist in magnifying their achievements and appropriating credit for the accomplishments of others.

They hold the belief of their own superiority and consistently fail to acknowledge the needs and emotions of others.

They will exercise a monopolistic control over any conversation and deride your perspective in the course of doing so.

They consistently anticipate receiving preferential treatment and exploit others to attain their objectives.

They consistently exhibit feelings of envy towards others and hold the belief that others harbor envy towards them.

They persist in demanding the highest quality in all aspects and asserting their preferences above all others—such as the finest automobile without regard for others' choices.

How it all began

In the period just prior to the outbreak of the Covid-19 pandemic, I received a kind invitation from an acquaintance from my college days to pay a visit to a married couple named Tope and Tola. Having resided in Canada for a considerable period of time, our friend expressed optimism about their ability to assist us in assimilating more effectively into the Canadian way of life. Tope cordially extended a warm welcome to us upon our arrival at his residence, demonstrating genuine interest in our academic pursuits and offering counsel regarding his favored immigration route. Tope apprised us that he and his spouse migrated to Canada three years ago. Upon the culmination of our visit, he presented me with the church flyer and extended a cordial invitation to attend the forthcoming church service.

Despite having already found a Nigerian church, I opted to accept Tope's invitation in order to assess my level of comfort at each of the churches.

By chance, it happened to be the birthday of the Pastor's spouse, consequently resulting in an extended church service accompanied by a generous array of refreshments, predominantly consisting of Nigerian culinary offerings. This was my initial attendance at such a gathering in Canada after a period of three months. It was exciting. I was home.

In the aftermath of this remarkable initial gathering, Pastor Ola and his spouse, Tayo, reached out to me on multiple occasions to express gratitude for my presence, inquire about my educational pursuits, and extend a warm invitation to join them in fellowship once more. I liked this church. In addition to the fact that the majority of them shared my native language (Yoruba), they exhibited pleasant and authentically affable dispositions. In Nigeria, I had never previously experienced the intimate setting of a small church. Consequently, this unique experience fostered a sense of unity and familial connection among the congregation.

Upon my third attendance at the recently inaugurated church, I received a gracious invitation from Pastor Ola and his spouse to join them in their domicile. The couple exhibited a great deal of hospitality and appeared genuinely invested in assisting those in their vicinity. During the course of the visit, I conversed with Tayo about the challenges I encountered with my accommodations. I conveyed to her that I had conducted a thorough examination of several locations, and she proposed the idea of visiting an acquaintance of ours from Nigeria to inquire about the possibility of renting her basement, presenting an alternative choice for me. I complied and she expeditiously contacted the acquaintance, and we promptly embarked on our journey.

On our way to her friend's house, Tayo asked if I had family joining me in Canada, and I told her I was divorced and hinted about the bad experience it had been. She expressed her empathy towards me, which served as a catalyst for a more extensive discourse on the lack of accountability exhibited by certain individuals of the male gender.

The statement that followed took me aback. She made accusations against Deola, the spouse of one of the church members, suggesting that he was lacking in responsibility. Furthermore, she expressed her bewilderment at why Deola's spouse chose to remain in the relationship with him.

Additionally, she asserted that in the event of any circumstances arising between her and her husband, Pastor Ola, she would promptly seek a divorce.

I was puzzled by this statement, yet I did not attach much significance to it, as I had grown accustomed to hearing Nigerian women discuss their husbands in a comparable manner. I have perpetually pondered why individuals discuss divorce in such a nonchalant manner - I was compelled to proceed with it as it was the sole recourse available to me, not because it was my desire.

After a considerable span of time, I gradually comprehended that her perception of an ideal husband encapsulated an individual who assumed full financial responsibility and unquestioningly acceded to all requests posed by his spouse, regardless of their propriety or validity. Upon reflecting upon that interaction, it has become apparent to me that I disregarded a number of warning signs. What could be the reason for her sharing details about another individual's personal relationship with me, given that it had only been three weeks since we met? This already indicated indications of an individual prone to sharing stories and divulging information about others without reservation.

I have come to recognize that it was during that particular instance when I should have made a decision regarding the type of information I would impart to her in the future. In hindsight, had I done so, it would have alleviated a significant amount of suffering. However, it marked the commencement of her efforts to elicit confidential details about my personal life. Details which she would later exploit as a means to harm me.

Upon contemplation and during the process of recuperating from the extensive emotional turmoil in which I found myself entangled a year ago, I found myself pondering the actions I might have taken had I approached the situation differently. One of the initial options that emerged in my thoughts was to adopt a more elusive and exceedingly careful approach. On certain occasions, removing oneself from the equation at an early stage could potentially serve as a means of safeguarding oneself. Unbeknownst to me, I was unwittingly entangled in an intricately crafted scheme designed to humiliate, deceive, and exert control over an unsuspecting individual – specifically, her husband!

Inherently, I possess a natural inclination towards empathy, sensitivity, and groundedness, which drives me to recognize the inherent capacity for brilliance in every individual I encounter. Being attuned to others' emotions can have both positive and negative consequences, bestowing both benefits and drawbacks. On occasion, individuals may appear naive and vulnerable, making them susceptible to exploitation. I am asserting this viewpoint as I have discerned numerous indicators that I regrettably failed to recognize. In my earnest pursuit to establish a sense of belonging in Canada, I allowed myself to be swayed by the conviction that my newly found religious community was beyond reproach.

My grounded disposition facilitates positive interpersonal relationships, fostering connections that may even warrant the title of friendship. The inquiry pertains to the extent of individuals who perceive me as their companion. In my personal circumstances, attaining obscurity could have proven insurmountable, as I was in the nascent stages of acquainting myself with the fellow individuals who were similarly compelled into an unfavourable predicament, one that should have never come to pass.

Authentic resilience manifests in having the courage to disengage from meaningless distractions.

When confronted by someone who initiates a contentious debate in order to assert their standpoint, and you possess a discernible awareness of an imminent whirlwind, do not allow yourself to be ensnared. Had I been aware of the individual's background, I would have refrained from interacting with her. I acted solely on the assumption that we had established a friendship and believed that any conflict between us could be effectively addressed.

I believe individuals would refrain from purposefully maintaining relationships with those who consistently expose them to circumstances that jeopardize their serenity. I have acquired the skill of keenly observing the individuals in my vicinity. What observations have I made? Not all individuals can be regarded as true companions; the majority of them conceal their malevolent intentions.

It is only one's adversary who seeks to inflict hurt and damage, as opposed to one's companion. While their objective may revolve around consistently being correct, it is imperative to note that this goal does not align with yours. The pursuit of absolute correctness is often overly emphasized and, ultimately, fails to possess sufficient value or warrant the investment of your valuable time. Maintaining a sense of tranquility offers a more valuable gratification.

Dialectical Behavior Therapy

This treatment modality has demonstrated significant efficacy in addressing personality disorders, anxiety disorders, depressive disorders, and post-traumatic stress disorder (PTSD). The majority of skills acquired during the course of the treatment possess applicability that extends to a diverse range of individuals. The majority of the advantages are applicable to everyday existence. Outlined below are several recommendations that can assist you in enhancing your ability to be fully present, effectively regulate your emotions, and actively participate by employing four straightforward techniques.

Whether you are an average person or experiencing a challenging situation, understanding the benefits of undergoing Dialectical Behavioral Therapy (DBT) can significantly enhance your everyday functioning. If you do not possess prior experience with or are presently undergoing treatment, what actions can you undertake? Presented below are several straightforward methods to initiate the utilization of certain components of Dialectical Behavior Therapy (DBT):

- Cease the playback of music.

Your preferred activity could potentially involve the enjoyment of music during the act of recreational vehicle navigation. This stands in contrast to the appropriate course of action. Engaging in diversions can be enjoyable, yet it has the potential to cause one to overlook matters of significance. What is the harm? It is conceivable that individuals may assert that the act of listening to music while operating a vehicle could potentially result in an increased likelihood of automobile collisions. It could potentially hinder your ability to be aware of your surroundings.

• Identify emotions experienced during a conversation

Each individual has encountered feelings of distress, although the underlying causes may remain elusive to some. In situations where the cause of one's emotional distress is unclear, it becomes challenging to take remedial action. This is the juncture at which the use of Dialectical Behavior Therapy (DBT) becomes applicable. It fosters individuals in enhancing their capacity to cultivate self-awareness regarding their actions, cognitions, and affect, thereby equipping them with the means to effectively regulate them. Although it may appear intricate, in reality, it is not. Being able to name emotions is a wonderful place to begin and a good place to practice is in daily conversations. "You graciously accepted the invitation to join us for dinner: "I am delighted that you have honored us with your presence at the dinner." "If your husband comes home late again: "I become agitated when you arrive home late without prior notification."

- Attentive listening • Engaged listening • Responsive listening • Focused listening • Concentrated listening

This may appear straightforward, yet have you ever found yourself contemplating your response prior to the completion of the interlocutor's utterance? Every individual is culpable of this. Occasionally, such circumstances may arise due to the intensity of the discussion or our heightened state of anxiety. Regardless of the option chosen, the outcome is destined to be unfavorable. Either you will utter words that you will ultimately feel remorseful about, or you will fail to attain your desired outcome.

While it is not necessary for you to concur with their viewpoints, I am not suggesting that you alter your perspective. However, the ability to genuinely listen has the potential to enhance your chances of attaining the intended objective. By engaging in active listening, you enhance the probability of the individual perceiving that their thoughts and emotions are being acknowledged, thereby increasing the likelihood of fulfilling your desired outcome. It is essential to consistently engage in attentive listening during conversations, regardless of internal inclination or personal preference.

- Reflect upon the value and significance of this matter.

You are likely familiar with the expression "engaging in futile efforts". This expression evokes the image of gerbils engaged in futile exertion on a spinning wheel. They do not move from their current location, yet they persistently engage in running. In times of distress, it is not uncommon to experience a loss of emotional equilibrium, causing one's thoughts and actions to become frenzied and unmanageable. One may encounter the frustration of becoming distressed over inconsequential matters.

During a moment of intense emotion, one might experience impaired rationality. Typically, you display an inclination towards fixating on your grievances, which ultimately leads to your personal distress and unhappiness. You can't tolerate stress.

If you find yourself in this situation, you are unable to undertake any actions that would contribute to its improvement. Frequently, your actions will exacerbate the situation, thereby perpetuating the ongoing cycle. Engaging in authentic self-expression hinders one's ability to perceive the inefficacy of their recurrent behaviors. The most straightforward approach to interrupt this process is to recognize and acknowledge intense emotional distress in oneself. Pause for a moment and inquire: "Does the value of this warrant investment?" "Do I possess any measure of influence?" "Is my response contributing to the improvement of the circumstances?"

The fundamental message conveyed by DBT is rather evident—you must assume responsibility for your own life and possess the capacity to effect personal transformations.

EMDR Therapy

Eye Movement Desensitization and Reprocessing therapy, a form of psychotherapy, serves to mitigate the emotional distress arising from traumatic memories. We shall now provide a concise elucidation of the essence of EMDR. It is highly advised against attempting this endeavor independently. This form of therapy necessitates the expertise of a qualified therapist.

This therapeutic approach strategically blends multiple components to optimize the efficacy of the treatment. This therapeutic approach involves focusing on three temporal dimensions: the past, the present, and the future. Emphasis is placed on past memories of a perturbing nature. The current scenario bestows upon you a source of distress while simultaneously fostering the acquisition of competencies necessary for forthcoming endeavors. "These issues are systematically addressed through an eight-phase treatment protocol:

Phase 1: This phase pertains to an exploration of your background. The initial EMDR processing may potentially shift your focus towards events experienced during your childhood rather than primarily addressing stressors encountered in adulthood. Clients acquire a comprehensive understanding of their circumstances and the factors causing them distress, prompting them to undergo transformative change. The duration of their treatment is influenced by the extent and timing of the trauma that led to the development of post-traumatic stress disorder. Individuals who have experienced a singular occurrence can receive treatment within an approximate time frame of five hours.

Extended treatment durations are necessary for individuals with multiple traumas.

Phase 2: During this stage, the therapist endeavors to ensure that the client possesses a diverse range of coping mechanisms to effectively manage distress. They will educate their clients on strategies for stress reduction that can be implemented both during and in the interim periods between treatments. The objective of Eye Movement Desensitization and Reprocessing (EMDR) is to facilitate efficient and accelerated transformation, ensuring that the individual maintains a foundation of stability throughout the course of treatment and in the intervals between sessions.

During phases 3 to 6, the identification and processing of a specific target take place. "The client is required to designate three elements:

An evocative depiction associated with the recollection

Unfavorable perception of oneself

Sensations of the body and corresponding emotions

The client will further discern optimistic convictions. The therapist will assist the client in assessing their positive belief while also evaluating the intensity of their negative emotions. The client is instructed to direct their attention towards an imagery, bodily sensations, and negative cognitions during the course of EMDR therapy.

Phase 7: During this stage, the therapist will request that the client maintain a comprehensive record of any pertinent content that may arise throughout the week. It serves as a reminder to the client of the coping techniques they acquired during the second phase, which assist in promoting a sense of inner calm.

Phase 8: Commencing the client's upcoming session will involve the initiation of phase eight. This phase entails reflecting upon the progress made thus far. The EMDR thoroughly engages with all past occurrences, present occurrences, and potential future occurrences that may necessitate diverse reactions.

Mitigating The Effects Of Gaslighting From A Disparaging Acquaintance

Your social network can serve as a potent source of support that uplifts you during times of difficulty. However, they can also assume the role of the chief instigator for your perplexity by means of consistently vilifying, engaging in gossip, issuing severe denunciations, employing shaming techniques, and resorting to manipulative guilt-tripping tactics. Given our inherent expectations for affection, assistance, and integrity from individuals in our innermost circles, it may prove to be a challenge to promptly recognize acts of manipulation perpetrated by our acquaintances.

Gaslighting individuals within one's social circle can subject them to feelings of shame regarding their decisions and create a sense of isolation, thereby distancing them from individuals who possess the ability to foster feelings of empowerment. As long as they succeed in convincing you that your perspectives are subordinate to their own, they maintain the ability to manipulate you according to their desires. If you find yourself compelled to seek approval from individuals who consistently undermine your self-worth, it is an indication that they have already assumed a controlling role in your life.

If you consistently find yourself reliant on a friend's decision-making, consistently seeking their approval prior to making personal choices, or feeling incapable of engaging in socially acceptable behaviors without their guidance, despite experiencing genuine dissatisfaction in their company, it is possible that you are maintaining a friendship with a gaslighting individual or a "frenemy."

If confidential information you share with them is transformed into public content for mockery, it indicates that you have encountered a friend who engages in gaslighting behavior. An individual who derives enjoyment from spreading rumors about you and derives satisfaction from your miseries is exhibiting clear indications of engaging in gaslighting. They express a desire for you to engage in a conflict with acquaintances, a conflict that they actively provoke.

What course of action would be appropriate to take when dealing with a friend who engages in gaslighting behaviors?

Initially, it is imperative to maintain a distance from them. A possible approach is to be candid about the matter and decisively withdraw. Sever all connections, communicate your disinterest in continuing their company, and assertively convey your resolution. Making this decision may prove challenging, however, it is imperative that you detach yourself from their harmful influence by removing them from your life. Take proactive measures to avoid being discarded by the gaslighter once they tire of manipulating you. You possess a higher value than what is currently being recognized. Why postpone until the moment they no longer have any utility for you? Why allow an individual to inundate your existence with superfluous dramatics when you possess the capability to take action against it?

An alternative approach to terminating the friendship would involve adopting a notably dull and uninteresting demeanor, prompting the gaslighter to naturally distance themselves from the relationship. Individuals who engage in gaslighting behaviors have a propensity for inducing distress and disorienting others. However, adopting an ambivalent stance as a response can deplete their energy swiftly and divert their attention away from you. An alternative approach would involve refraining from becoming defensive in response to an inflammatory comment made by the individual employing gaslighting techniques. Instead, one could opt to reply with phrases like "I understand," "Perhaps," or "Very well," among others. Exhibit intentional and unwavering behavior, and in due course, your friend who engages in gaslighting will perceive you as exceedingly tedious.

Irrespective of the level of intimacy that exists between you and a friend who engages in gaslighting behavior, should you reach a decision to terminate the harmful mistreatment, it is imperative to resolve never to engage in any form of financial transactions, such as borrowing or lending, with them. Decline any gifts and reject any forms of assistance extended to you. A gaslighter possesses a persistent ability to ensure that their ostensibly benevolent gestures ensnare and plague you. They might even go as far as making accusations of theft against you. This is among their myriad strategies for seeking retribution if they perceive that you have transgressed against them. Furthermore, should you choose to extend them any form of assistance, it would be prudent not to anticipate its return. To prevent potential negative repercussions, it is advisable to refrain from engaging in any form of exchange with them.

A friend who engages in gaslighting demonstrates a lack of genuine concern for your well-being and the things that hold significance in your life. Do not entrust them with the responsibility of caring for your children, pets, and possessions under any circumstances. Gaslighters possess the capability to inflict irreparable harm upon you.

Furthermore, they have the capability to refute any such actions and manipulate your perception, leading you to believe that it is merely a figment of your imagination. In formal tone: An individual engaging in gaslighting may forcefully disavow any responsibility for a certain action of which you are confident they are guilty, subsequently shifting the blame onto you for making unfounded accusations. They might express their concern by stating, "In what manner could you endanger the integrity of our friendship through such serious allegations?" You have permitted your unfounded conjectures to become overly exaggerated, and I cannot remain present to engage with this unfounded discourse!"

Etiology, Clinical Manifestations, And Consequences

Factors Contributing to Codependency

Codependency does not stem from inherent flaws in one's character or personality, nor is it linked to genetic predispositions. It is an acquired behavior that typically begins at a young age in an individual's life. The subsequent elements are correlated with the emergence of codependent patterns.

Coping with a Family Member Afflicted by a Mental or Physical Condition

Individuals who have dedicated a substantial portion of their lives to the provision of care for a chronically ill family member have a heightened susceptibility to developing a codependent relationship. They acquire the ability to prioritize the needs of the ill individual over their own and display remarkable levels of personal selflessness. Over a period of time, these caregivers may gradually neglect their own personal needs in order to meet the requirements of their ailing family member. Ultimately, individuals have the capacity to subconsciously reconfigure their mental processes in order to derive their self-esteem from the compassion they are able to exhibit. Assuming complete accountability for the welfare of the afflicted individual transforms into an all-consuming preoccupation, resembling a means of exerting authority.

Experiencing a Challenging Childhood due to Parental Dysfunction

Adults who were brought up in households characterized by parental drug abuse or substance misuse are prone to exhibiting codependent characteristics. Coming of age in such households and witnessing firsthand how their parents' irresponsible conduct compelled the children to assume caregiving duties prematurely. Furthermore, as a result of enduring incessant severe criticisms, mistreatment, harassment, and disregard, the children acquire the inclination to prioritize their parents' needs over their own. They develop the belief that prioritizing the well-being of others overrides self-care. Such forms of influence profoundly shape a child's psychological growth and may consequently result in the inclination towards seeking interdependent and impaired relationships in adulthood.

Maturing in a Dysfunctional Household

The occurrence of physical, emotional, and sexual abuse can give rise to profoundly traumatizing experiences in young children. Children who are raised in households characterized by frequent instances of abuse are prone to enduring the lifelong repercussions of such traumatic experiences. It is not infrequent for individuals with this background to form imbalanced and harmful relationships in adulthood, as this aligns with their subconscious perception of a relationship.

Individuals raised in abusive households often develop the ability to suppress or silence their emotions of anger and frustration as a means to endure the distress caused by their traumatic encounters. If this behavior persists into their adulthood, it is probable that they will develop codependent tendencies.

Indications of Codependency.

The subsequent information can assist in assessing whether you exhibit codependent behaviors or are engaged in a codependent relationship.

Low Self-esteem

Generally, an individual exhibiting codependent tendencies tends to perceive themselves as inadequate. They endure a profound awareness of their shortcomings, consistently experiencing feelings of shame and guilt. These indicators are indicative of diminished self-regard. In order to surmount this sensation of inadequacy, individuals with codependency tendencies exert significant efforts to demonstrate their worthiness of love and necessity. This mindset may lead to an unwholesome preoccupation with the needs, problems, and feelings of others.

If one discovers oneself excessively concerned about being physically inadequate, lacking the necessary qualifications, or lacking sufficient worthiness for their partner, it is probable that they are dependent on their partner for their self-esteem.

Overreacting to Personal Matters and Exhibiting a Strong Sensitivity towards Critique

Individuals who exhibit codependency tendencies typically demonstrate a proclivity for defensiveness and are prone to perceiving opposing viewpoints or disagreements as potential threats. Due to their propensity for struggling to establish and sustain firm personal boundaries, they tend to readily internalize situations and predominantly function in a reactive manner.

They also exhibit a high degree of sensitivity towards criticism. Codependents have been subjected to accountability, emotional pain, and censuring throughout the majority of their existence. They swiftly absorb the perspectives of others and conflate these viewpoints with an accurate portrayal of their own identity. In an effort to preempt criticism, individuals with codependency tendencies rigorously strive to avert conflicts, appease others (even in inconvenient situations), and strive to minimize visibility to evade unwarranted scrutiny and potential censure.

Sustained Abandonment of Individual Interests and Emotions

Codependents hold the belief that by disregarding their genuine emotions, they will eventually dissipate. However, this ultimately engenders feelings of resentment. As they prioritize the emotions and well-being of others over their own, they endure a persistent state of self-sacrifice and subjugation of their own sentiments.

Similarly, they fail to acknowledge their difficulties. Conversely, individuals perceive their dependent as the one facing the issue and endeavor to remedy the situation. Despite forming new relationships, codependents cannot resolve their issues until they acknowledge that the source of the problem lies within themselves rather than external factors.

If an individual or acquaintances demonstrate a tendency to prioritize the feelings and concerns of others over their own, it may indicate the presence of codependency.

Lack of assertiveness in expressing their needs and desires

Due to their concern for the feelings of others, many individuals identified as codependents may often find it challenging to express their desires and needs precisely. Manipulation appears to be the favored means through which they convey their wants and wishes to individuals they hold affection for. However, it is often the case that individuals will suppress their desires and feign contentment, which serves as a harbinger of impending frustration.

If one tends to exhibit cautious behavior in the presence of specific individuals, it is indicative of a potential codependency in one's relationship with them. If you are perpetually consumed by the apprehension that your honesty might provoke displeasure in your significant other, it is probable that you are engaged in a codependent association with them. If the interpersonal exchange within your relationship lacks transparency and is characterized by the dominance of fear, it serves as a manifestation of codependent tendencies.

Striving for Validation via Compliant Conduct

Partners in mutually supportive relationships strive to satisfy each other's needs within appropriate boundaries, which is deemed acceptable. Nevertheless, a codependent partner holds the belief that they are obligated to satisfy the needs and desires of their partner. There are two underlying motivations behind their actions: firstly, seeking validation from their partner, and secondly, deriving a sense of personal satisfaction. Codependents perceive their self-worth exclusively through the act of bringing happiness to others, thus resorting to people-pleasing behaviors.

Codependent individuals exhibit a tendency to engage in people-pleasing behavior, manifesting in their consistent agreement to meet every request made by their partner. An individual who experiences feelings of unease when refusing a request from their partner or a loved one is exhibiting indications of codependent behavior. They are relinquishing their authority and forfeiting their sense of self as they prioritize interpersonal connections above their individual empowerment.

An illustrative instance of individuals prioritizing the approval of others is when an individual hesitates to decline sexual propositions from their partner despite having no desire to engage in sexual activity. Given their challenges with effective communication, individuals with codependency tendencies often acquiesce to nearly any request from their loved ones in order to sidestep potential conflicts. It is not infrequent for individuals in codependent relationships to experience a sense of aversion towards their partner, yet still engage in sexual activities with them solely for the purpose of appeasing them.

NARCISSIST AND FAME

Their primary motivation lies in attaining widespread recognition and acclaim. Celebrity status entails several significant roles: it bestows the narcissist with authority, furnishes a perpetual wellspring of Narcissistic Supply (e.g., admiration, adoration, approval, and astonishment), and satisfies crucial aspects of the individual's Ego.

The perception that the narcissist projects is reciprocated and mirrored by those who come into contact with his or her notoriety or renown. In this manner, he experiences a sense of vitality, his very being is validated, and he attains a distinct perception of boundaries (delimiting the narcissist from the external world).

The pursuit of fame is often accompanied by a range of narcissistic behaviors. The narcissist exhibits a near absence of inhibitions, displaying a willingness to transgress nearly all boundaries in their relentless pursuit of fame and notoriety. In his perspective, negative publicity holds no significance. What truly matters is capturing public attention and remaining visible.

As the narcissist derives equal satisfaction from various forms of attention and finds pleasure in being both feared and loved, there is an indifference on their part towards the accuracy of public information about them, as long as their name is spelled correctly. The narcissist experiences negative emotional episodes solely when faced with periods of insufficient attention, publicity, or exposure.

The narcissist subsequently experiences a sense of inner void, depletion, insignificance, humiliation, anger, perception of discrimination, lack of privileges, neglect, and feelings of being treated unfairly, among others. Initially, he endeavors to garner attention from progressively diminishing subsets of reference (or "reducing the scale of supply"). However, the sensation of compromising eats away at his already tenuous self-worth.

In due course, the advent of spring becomes evident. The individual of narcissistic disposition engages in strategizing, devising schemes, formulating plans, colluding, reflecting, evaluating, integrating information, and undertaking any other requisite actions to regain the vanished prominence in the public sphere.

As his ability to captivate the target demographic (typically the largest) diminishes, his approach grows increasingly audacious, unconventional, and extraordinary. The unwavering resolve to establish a public presence gives way to determined implementation, eventually transitioning into an anxious cycle of seeking attention through various behaviors.

The narcissist does not possess genuine interest in publicity itself. Narcissists are misleading. The narcissist displays an apparent self-admiration, while deep down, he harbors self-loathing. In a parallel manner, he seems to possess an inclination towards attaining celebrity status, and in actuality, his preoccupation lies in the responses elicited by his fame. People actively observe him, take notice of him, engage in discussions about him, and deliberate over his actions, thereby asserting his existence.

The narcissist actively seeks out and gathers the various mannerisms that people exhibit upon noticing him. He positions himself as the focal point of attention, or even as a figure that elicits controversy. He persistently and repeatedly annoys his closest acquaintances in an attempt to confirm that he has not lost his renown, his inherent talent, or the regard of his social circle.

Indeed, it is evident that the narcissist is not discerning in their choices. If he attains fame as a writer, he engages in writing; if as a businessman, he undertakes commercial activities. He transitions seamlessly between different domains without any sense of regret, as he remains steadfast in each endeavor, driven solely by the determination to achieve fame, which he believes he is entitled to.

He evaluates activities, hobbies, and individuals based on their usefulness rather than the pleasure they provide him. His judgment is driven by their potential to enhance his reputation and the degree to which they can do so. The narcissist possesses a single-minded focus (without exaggerating, we could describe it as obsessive). His existence resides within the dichotomy of obscurity and renown, where the spectrum spans from being unnoticed and uncharted to being hailed and exalted.

When it comes to the perspective of their fans, celebrities serve two emotional purposes: they offer a mythical storyline that fans can associate themselves with and serve as receptacles where fans can project their aspirations, apprehensions, intentions, principles, and longings, effectively fulfilling their wishes. Even the slightest departure from these prescribed roles triggers substantial anger and instills within us a desire to penalize (publicly shame) these "non-conforming" public figures.

But why?

When the inherent flaws, susceptibilities, and weaknesses of a public figure come to light, the admirer experiences a sense of embarrassment, a feeling of being deceived, a loss of optimism, and a void within themselves. In order to reaffirm their sense of self-value, the supporter must establish their moral ascendancy over the flawed and "sinful" celebrity. The fan is required to impart a valuable lesson to the celebrity and assert their dominance. This can be regarded as a rudimentary defensive mechanism characterized by narcissistic grandiosity. It places the fan on a level playing field with the vulnerable and unguarded celebrity.

There exists an inherent delight in the infliction of pain and a perverse intrigue in observing the anguish of others from a distance. The act of being spared the sufferings and hardships that others endure instills in the observer a sense of being "selected," protected, and morally upright. As a celebrity's fame and influence continue to escalate, their descent becomes increasingly steep. There is a certain satisfaction derived from witnessing the defiance and subsequent retribution of hubris.

Disparaging public figures or reveling in their downfall is akin to the contemporary rendition of the ancient gladiatorial arena.

Gossip once served a comparable purpose, whereas now the mass media airs the live depiction of the demise of revered deities. Revenge is not a factor in this situation - only the experience of Schadenfreude, the moral conflict of experiencing pleasure in observing your superiors being penalized and humbled.

Narcissistic individuals exhibit sadistic tendencies, are ambitious, lack empathy, possess a self-righteous demeanor, demonstrate pathological and destructive envy, and potentially harbor fluctuating self-worth issues, which may be indicative of an underlying inferiority complex.

In the context of the fans, the capacity to engage in the vicarious experience of the celebrity's remarkable (and often partly fictitious) lifestyle. The famous individual assumes the role of their "delegate" in the realm of imagination, their extension and representative, the manifestation and personification of their innermost longings and covert aspirations. Numerous public figures also serve as exemplary models or parental figures. Celebrities serve as tangible evidence that life encompasses more than monotonous and repetitive routines. It is undeniable that individuals who possess remarkable beauty, or rather flawless features, do indeed exist and furthermore, they tend to lead seemingly enchanted existences. There is still reason for optimism - this is the sentiment conveyed by the celebrity to his/her supporters.

The celebrity's inexorable decline and moral deterioration serves as a contemporary parallel to the medieval genre of morality plays. This course of events — transitioning from poverty to wealth and recognition, and then experiencing a decline back to poverty or even worse circumstances — demonstrates the prevailing nature of order and justice, the inevitable retribution that accompanies excessive pride, and the notion that celebrities are no more virtuous or esteemed than their followers.

The origins of pathological narcissism remain elusive, as it is uncertain whether it stems from innate predispositions, the adverse consequences of abusive and traumatic upbringing, or a combination thereof. Frequently, within the confines of a single family unit, characterized by shared parents and an indistinguishable emotional atmosphere, certain siblings may manifest as malignant narcissists, while others exhibit typical, non-pathological behavior. Undoubtedly, this signifies a inherent genetic inclination in certain individuals towards the development of narcissism. Based on the available evidence, it would be prudent to infer that individuals with narcissistic tendencies may possess an inherent inclination towards developing narcissistic defense mechanisms, although concrete substantiation thereof is currently lacking. These conditions are induced by mistreatment or distress experienced in the developmental period of infancy or early adolescence.

Within the context of "abuse," I am alluding to a range of behaviors that commodify the child, perceiving them as an appendage of the caregiver (parent) or as a mere means of satisfaction. Engaging in acts of excessive control and suffocation can be just as detrimental as physical abuse and deprivation. Illicit treatment can be inflicted not only by peers, but also by parental figures or adult influencers.

An ample number of celebrities do not exhibit narcissistic tendencies. However, it is evident that a portion of them are indeed so.

We each strive to perceive affirmative indications from our fellow individuals. These cues serve to bolster specific behavioral tendencies within us. It is not particularly remarkable that the narcissistic celebrity engages in similar behavior. Nevertheless, there exist two prominent distinctions between the narcissistic and the typical personality.

The initial aspect pertains to quantities.

The average individual is prone to appreciating a moderate level of attention, both spoken and non-verbal, in the form of affirmation, approval, or admiration. Excessive levels of attention, however, are commonly regarded as burdensome and actively evaded.

Destructive and adverse criticism is completely disregarded.

On the other hand, the narcissist exemplifies the psychological equivalent of an individual struggling with alcoholism. He is insatiable. He consciously directs his entire conduct, indeed his entire existence, towards acquiring these gratifying morsels of attention. He incorporates them within a cohesive, entirely subjective representation of his own persona. He employs them as a means of managing his volatile sense of self-worth and self-esteem.

In order to sustain continuous intrigue, the narcissist disseminates a fabricated and fictitious portrayal of oneself onto others, commonly referred to as the False Self. The pseudo personality encompasses traits and qualities that are in stark contrast to those of the narcissist: possessing supreme knowledge, unlimited power, captivating charisma, exceptional intellect, vast wealth, or extensive social ties.

The narcissist subsequently proceeds to obtain responses to this projected image from individuals within their family, social circle, professional network, immediate community, and professional acquaintances. If the aforementioned expressions of adoration, reverence, recognition, trepidation, esteem, ovation, and validation are not present, the narcissist insists upon or coerces their manifestation. Currency, praise, a positive evaluation, media recognition, and a conquest of one's desires all undergo an equivalent conversion process within the narcissist's cognitive framework, resulting in what is known as 'narcissistic supply'.

Therefore, the narcissist does not possess a genuine inclination towards seeking publicity or attaining fame. Indeed, his primary focus lies in the responses elicited by his renown: the manner in which individuals observe, acknowledge, discuss, and analyze his conduct. It serves to demonstrate his own existence.

The narcissist meticulously observes and gathers the subtle transformations in people's facial expressions when they become aware of his presence. He positions himself as the focal point of attention, or even assumes the role of a contentious figure.

He consistently and repeatedly bothers those who are closest to him in an attempt to reassure himself that he is not losing his prestige, his talent, or the attention of his social circle.

CHAPTER 2

Returning to the passages in 2 Timothy, we find that narcissism is addressed within this context. Upon further examination of the aforementioned nine characteristics, it becomes evident that all of them are encompassed within the scriptures presented herein.

In this passage, Paul cautions Timothy to exercise caution when dealing with individuals who exhibit self-centered tendencies. One cannot bring a sense of self-love into a relationship and anticipate its success.

He states, "However, it is important to acknowledge that in the forthcoming era, there will be times of great danger and uncertainty." In a formal tone, an alternative way to express the same sentiment could be: "Men shall exhibit a tendency towards self-centeredness, an excessive fondness for material wealth, exhibitionism, arrogance, sacrilege, defiance of parental authority, ingratitude, impiety, lack of compassion, refusal to grant forgiveness, defamation, deficiency in self-discipline, brutality, disdain for divinity, treachery, obstinacy, arrogance, and a preference for hedonistic pursuits over devotion to the divine."

In the fifth verse, it is stated that "...". "Avail yourself the opportunity to distance yourself from such individuals" (NKJV) "Exercise caution and maintain a safe distance from these individuals" (MSG)

Upon witnessing Paul's inclination to "turn away," it appeared that he concurred with the content of secular literature I had perused on narcissism. These works consistently advocate for a sole course of action: the act of disconnecting oneself from the narcissistic individual. Every single one of them (and I have meticulously studied more than 30 books on narcissism), each publication has been authored with a secular framework, and each one unequivocally advocates for withdrawing oneself: terminate your marriage if you find yourself wedded to a narcissist, terminate your relationship if you find yourself entangled with a narcissist. If you are not currently married, I am inclined to support this proposed resolution, however, kindly remove yourself from the situation. However, if you are already married, it is not within my purview to instruct you to "get out" easily or without due consideration, as I must acknowledge the presence of divine principles. There are certain extenuating circumstances that must present themselves before I will have the courage to say to you 'get out'. However, in my capacity as a devoted follower of Christianity and a clergy member, it is incumbent upon me to express my inability to endorse the notion of simply advising you to depart, concurring with the all-encompassing secular resolution.

This comprehensive solution indicates that there exists a finite boundary to the extent of divine influence or transformation upon an individual. The meaning behind it suggests that there exist certain men and women who are beyond the reach of God's influence, which is something I find myself unable to embrace. Nobody is beyond God. According to the scriptures, it is written that He is the divine being who reigns over all living beings; no challenge is insurmountable for Him. Praise God!

Paul initiated an examination of the traits associated with narcissism. The term narcissism derives from the Greek mythology surrounding Narcissus, an exceedingly attractive individual who would habitually fixate upon his own reflection in a mirror. His physical appearance was exceptionally pleasing, leading him to develop a deep affection for himself. He was unable to tolerate the idea of parting with the mirror. He was excessively preoccupied with his appearance to the extent that he was unable to rouse himself to attend to basic necessities such as eating or hydrating. He ultimately perished, in the presence of his own reflection. And thus, the term narcissist originated from that very source.

This individual demonstrates an excessive self-centeredness and an overwhelming self-admiration, resulting in their disregard for others and their unwillingness to acknowledge others' needs or worthiness. Narcissism entails an excessive preoccupation with oneself.

Coping With Vindictive Behavior

Engaging in a relationship with an individual exhibiting symptoms of narcissistic personality disorder can prove to be quite demanding, particularly when their behavior takes on an acutely malicious nature. Regardless of whether they are your closest friend, coworker, family member, or life partner, there are certain actions you should take in order to ensure your personal safety:

1. Put down stopping points:

The primary approach to protecting oneself while involved in a relationship with an individual displaying Narcissistic Personality Disorder (NPD) is to establish "clear boundaries." It is crucial to articulate these boundaries by providing well-founded rationales that align with your personal beliefs.

An individual afflicted with the disorder may endeavor to convince you to modify your boundary. Remain steadfast. Given that any compromise you make will undoubtedly be advantageous to them, it is not advisable to engage in logical discussions with them. Similarly, it is prudent to consider upholding those boundaries, even when they pertain to individuals who are considered "family."

In situations where an individual within one's family exhibits vindictive narcissistic tendencies, it is not uncommon to experience a strong sense of obligation to maintain ties with them, as there exists a prevailing notion that family bonds are steadfast and unbreakable. We provide remarks such as, "However, that individual is my sibling" or "It is customary for our family to visit that place on Halloween."

To be frank, establishing this boundary with close relatives poses a challenge. In contrast, if there is no familial connection. However, it must be acknowledged that failing to establish boundaries is not only unsafe, but may also exacerbate mental health concerns within the family.

It is for this very reason that you ought to establish the parameters of your commitment with this individual exclusively with regard to your own safety and well-being.

2. Please specify your terms or limitations.

Articulating your viewpoint entails adhering to the prescribed guidelines and effectively communicating your boundaries and limitations. By defining your own conditions, individuals with NPD are given the chance to recognize, comprehend, or depart. Nevertheless, if they fail to acknowledge your boundaries, especially in malevolent manners, you are entitled to take any necessary measures to adequately protect yourself.

You have the potential to assert yourself and exude self-assurance. Make an effort to not allow their lack of respect towards you to pass without a response. By refraining from responding when they openly insult you or display impoliteness towards you, you are inadvertently endorsing their behavior.

3. Please refrain from second-guessing yourself.

When involved in a relationship with an individual who has Narcissistic Personality Disorder (NPD), it is common to experience a propensity for self-reflection and an inclination to excessively scrutinize oneself. This can be attributed to the fact that you have been subjected to deceptive tactics and manipulative maneuvers. In instances such as these, there exists a proclivity to forfeit your individual expression within the relationship and consistently rely on their superior discernment; as a consequence, this leads to a diminished sense of self-assurance.

4. Endeavor to exclude:

When an individual is displaying malevolent behavior, they may make assertions intended to portray you in a particular manner for a strategic objective. As an example, one might express this notion by stating, "You possess a propensity for sensitiveness" or "Your perceptions may be fantastical in nature."

Please take into consideration that they may be experiencing emotional distress and may be responding by trying to inflict harm upon you due to feeling threatened by your presence. It is imperative that you refrain from internalizing their words, as doing so would grant them a victory over you.

Instead, internalize and embrace positive affirmations about yourself.

Regardless of their behavior, it is important to remember that you are not to blame. Even if they attempt to manipulate you into believing otherwise, do not succumb to their deceptive tactics. Please be aware that they are affected by a condition that distorts their perception of you and others.

5. Cover up their outrage:

Exercise restraint when attempting to challenge or negate their viewpoints during instances of heightened emotional reactivity. One could perceive that the subject matter of their conversation is not morally appropriate. It is possible that this is the case, however, individuals diagnosed with Narcissistic Personality Disorder (NPD) typically exhibit a reluctance to accept responsibility for their actions. Seeking to convince them will merely lead to an escalation of the dispute. I understand that this can be extremely challenging, especially in the event that they have uttered something detrimental towards you. However, it is imperative that you seek refuge from their fury as your own wrath will not yield any constructive outcomes and could potentially result in physical harm.

6.Foster a security plan:
A vengeful individual with narcissistic tendencies is not invariably characterized by brutality. Although they may exhibit manipulative tendencies or display extreme reactions towards certain situations, it does not imply that they would necessarily launch an attack. However, if they have caused physical harm or made threatening gestures in the past, there is a high likelihood that they will repeat such behavior, and it will likely escalate in

severity. It is highly advisable to establish a secure plan for disengaging from the relationship.

In any situation where cruelty may potentially manifest, it is highly advisable to have a contingency plan in place. None of us possess the entitlement to resort to violence or demonstrate aggression towards another individual."

7.Think about requesting help:

It is commonplace to experience confusion and bewilderment upon disengaging from a relationship with an individual characterized by malevolent egotism. For the intended purposes, they can be considered as an acquaintance or a relative. It is permissible, however, to seek assistance and regular reassurance for navigating the dynamics of your relationship. It would be prudent to consult with various individuals close to you regarding the current experiences you are facing. Additionally, it may be necessary to contemplate seeking the guidance of a mental health professional for your own well-being.

Engaging in a relationship with an individual displaying narcissistic personality disorder can prove to be highly arduous and vexatious. Lack of well-defined and foreseeable boundaries can have a detrimental impact on your enduring friendships and overall emotional welfare.

A professional specializing in mental health or another qualified mental healthcare provider can aid you in devising practical recommendations to adjust to your emotions and the dynamics of your relationship. Undoubtedly, the consequences that persist after the termination of a relationship can bear significant implications for those who opt to depart.

8. Suggest that they also seek assistance: Therapeutic interventions exhibit the potential to engender transformative shifts in the interpersonal and intrapersonal dynamics of individuals with NPD. Moreover, such interventions may concomitantly mitigate the propensity for developing comorbid psychological afflictions. This includes:

tension turmoil

gloom/depression

substance use disorder

Nevertheless, be prepared to acknowledge and embrace the possibility that they may not adhere to your notion of offering assistance. Individuals diagnosed with Narcissistic Personality Disorder encounter difficulties in developing self-awareness regarding their behavioral patterns and seeking assistance. Some individuals do not adhere to the treatment regimen for a sufficient duration, thereby impeding the occurrence of enduring transformations within them.

It is indeed prudent to focus solely on fostering one's own emotional well-being.

Observing Narcissistic Behavior

Due to the narcissist's deeply entrenched sense of self-importance, they will display distinct traits that are intrinsic to the disorder. To begin with, they will exhibit a demeanor that may be deemed as haughty, disdainful, self-important, or pretentious. In addition, they will exhibit an excessive level of self-assurance, misleadingly claim achievements they have not actually attained, and assume an inflated sense of importance beyond what is evidently warranted.

The entirety of the boasting privileges pertain to the individual exhibiting narcissistic tendencies.

They exhibit an excessive inclination towards boasting. Their boasting tends to manifest in a discreet and cunning manner, in order to avoid appearing overt and blatant, as they strive to evade being caught making embellishments. They have the potential to excel in the art of self-promotion. The boasting will be resolute and persistent. If they possess verifiable accomplishments, they will consistently embellish the significance of said attainments. They will consistently present themselves as authorities on various matters, irrespective of their complete lack of knowledge on the subject matter.

The individual with narcissistic tendencies exhibits traits of a fantastical thinker.

Occasionally, the narcissist exhibits a phenomenon known as fantastical ideation surrounding their exceptional qualities, depth of knowledge, and capabilities to achieve. Some individuals may erroneously believe that their personal convictions and perceptions always align with objective reality, disregarding compelling evidence to the contrary. In instances where the narcissist's inability to match up to another person becomes evident, they tend to experience feelings of envy and exhibit both disdain and disapproval towards the individual in order to minimize their stature to the greatest extent possible.

The Entitled Narcissist

As per the assertions of the individual with narcissistic tendencies, they believe they possess the inherent right to obtain all their desires and expect that every circumstance in life should unfold according to their preferences. They are deserving of the utmost preferential treatment wherever they may travel, and it is imperative for all individuals to adhere to their desires, methods of execution, and cognitive perspective. The individual in question consistently assumes a position of superiority within the relationship, thus labeling anyone who fails to comply as a challenging, unintelligent, and socially uncomfortable individual in the narcissist's unique realm.

The Manipulating Narcissist

Frequently, individuals may find themselves compelled to assume a subordinate role as a result of their status as an employee, spouse, or offspring. Alternatively, on occasions, the individual in question may exhibit timidity and reticence, refraining from contesting the dominant will and authority of the narcissistic individual. The individual exhibiting narcissistic traits will commence each fresh interpersonal bond with the underlying assumption that the other party occupies a subordinate role, even in instances where this is not the case. This situates the narcissist in a circumstance wherein they can readily exploit individuals who happen to be in such an unfortunate situation.

The Multifarious Narcissists

These behaviors and attitudes encapsulate the psychological state of the individual exhibiting narcissistic tendencies. The condition can manifest in a spectrum of severity levels. Certain individuals with narcissistic tendencies exhibit such dysfunctional familial and social connections that they ultimately find themselves solitary, shattered, and incapable of societal integration. Some individuals possess the ability to proficiently employ strategies and tactics of manipulation, leading to considerable success in their careers or attaining top positions in their highly demanding fields. As a result, they accumulate a group of subordinates who cater to their every requirement, suppress their own pride, and typically enjoy significant financial rewards. Nevertheless, individuals with narcissistic tendencies tend to experience a consistent lack of success in various aspects of their lives. Their inability to maintain lasting relationships, in which love dictates one's actions, stems from their exclusive self-centeredness. They possess an eternal devotion to themselves, constantly fixated on their own reflection when peering into the pool.

TYPES OF NARCISSIST

Narcissism constitutes a personality trait that can manifest itself to varying degrees, such that the more pronounced it becomes, the greater the propensity for it to align with symptomatic clusters associated with a mental disorder. Nevertheless, it is important to acknowledge that not all individuals exhibiting a heightened level of narcissism are afflicted by a mental disorder that substantially impairs their overall well-being.

The following is an enumeration of the various categories of individuals exhibiting narcissistic tendencies. Frequently, it is possible to observe the presence of three to four of these characteristics within an individual simultaneously. Attempting to accurately identify a distinct category in an individual you are acquainted with can prove to be a highly precarious endeavor. This list is designed to provide a comprehensive perspective on the various categories of narcissism. It necessitates the expertise of a professional to accurately ascertain an individual's diagnosis of narcissistic personality disorder.

Dependent/Vulnerable/Covert

He demonstrates a limited enthusiasm towards his own identity, instead prioritizing his desire for material gain. This variant of narcissistic behavior is distinguished by feelings of despair, employment of sarcasm, propensity for criticizing others, and a prevailing sense of negativity or weight in their presence.

Hence, these individuals possess a sense of subtle superiority, juxtaposed with the awareness that this superiority is impracticable. Hence, it is imperative to acquire exceptional measures to offset this circumstance. Their penchant for seeking validation from others delineates their obsessive disposition.

He experiences a profound longing for affection and remains perpetually unsatiated. He is consistently deprived of sufficient love. He experiences apprehension towards being deserted and dismissed. The primary issue he faces is his inability to exhibit self-love and self-care, instead prioritizing the dispensation of what he perceives as love towards others in order to obtain their approval and affection. This form of affection is typically displayed through materialistic gestures such as presents or financial contributions, which are rather superficial in nature, as he is unable to express authentic love and genuine care.

It poses a stifling condition for his significant other. This individual possesses an excessively self-centered disposition that restricts your autonomy. They exhibit a highly controlling nature, persistently desiring to be closely associated with you, monitoring your movements and frequently contacting you via text or phone calls to ascertain your location. They harbor an expectation that their partners shall refrain from engaging in any other connections apart from the one they share, compelling them to distance themselves from their social circle and kin. Throughout the day, they will incessantly question your affection towards them, insinuating that your love for them falls short.

They have a tendency to exhibit introverted tendencies, displaying a calm demeanor and a proclivity towards avoiding social interactions.

Nevertheless, in an attempt to veil his perpetual emotions of self-loathing and inadequacy, the narcissist endeavors to indemnify himself by embellishing his traits, assuming a facade, and endeavoring to assimilate his persona with the revered individuals around him. Frequently, they attempt to rectify this by adopting a persona that starkly contrasts with their current emotional state.

They desire to experience a sense of individuality and prioritize their emotions over the needs or emotions of others. Their primary motivations stem from a deep-seated apprehension of being rejected and forsaken. A vulnerable narcissist fails to demonstrate genuine love or concern for others, instead employing emotional manipulation as a means to garner sympathy and attention.

They possess a steadfast desire to perceive themselves as distinctive and exhibit minimal, if any, sincere consideration towards the emotions of others. This individual, characterized by narcissism, exhibits a profound and insatiable longing for affection that remains unfulfilled.

Similar to an unfathomable abyss that remains perpetually empty. He holds the conviction that he is not adequately bestowed with affection, experiences transient joy when receiving attention from others, only to subsequently revert back to a sense of void where approval and affection are concerned.

Frequently, a vulnerable narcissist develops a dependency on engaging in sexual activity. They are capable of engaging in simultaneous relationships and exhibit no hesitation in patronizing sex workers. To those individuals, this is deemed acceptable as they perceive it as a necessity. This compulsion can escalate to such an extent that individuals abandon their ethical principles in pursuit of a semblance of companionship.

The foundation of this disposition is rooted in a profound apprehension of being forsaken and dismissed, prompting the narcissist to tightly hold onto reliance. In order to fulfill those needs, he exhibits a complete disregard for ethical principles by employing manipulation tactics on individuals. His partner and close friends are expending emotional energy in an effort to nurture, console, and sustain his profound need for affection, which is steadily intensifying.

According to them, their life is in turmoil solely due to external circumstances, rather than acknowledging any personal responsibility for the difficulties they face.

They display a lack of awareness or concern for any distress you may be experiencing, as their preoccupations primarily revolve around self-pity. To the extent that they do express interest, it is driven by ulterior motives aimed at exploiting the situation.

This specific category of narcissist poses a notable threat due to the covert nature of their narcissistic tendencies. It is imperative not to judge this individual solely based on their superficial traits. They will employ any means necessary, both in their spoken words and actions, in order to attain their desired goals from you. They will employ excessive flattery and manipulation in order to win your affection, but should they not receive what they desire, they will subsequently resort to maintaining a deliberate silence. This practice is employed with the intention of invoking compassion from others, prompting them to hasten to their aid. That is when they have successfully maneuvered you into a position that aligns with their desired outcome.

The susceptible narcissist continually seeks sympathy and seeks reassurance that the blame does not lie with them, even when they are entirely responsible for the situation. They are unable to perceive or acknowledge their own accountability in the potentiality that their adversity is indeed a consequence of their actions. That they were responsible for it. Typically, individuals tend to attribute blame onto others who bear no responsibility whatsoever.

The vulnerable narcissists possess unwavering faith in the certainty of their own opinions and face significant difficulty in acknowledging or taking into account the perspectives of others. Identifying them is a straightforward task as their conversations consistently revolve around themselves, directing attention solely towards their desires. On each occasion when you endeavor to address an issue of personal concern, you ascertain that your voice goes unheard or is intentionally disregarded. This individual with narcissistic tendencies frequently interjects while others are speaking, often diverting the topic of discussion to unrelated matters.

The sole method of safeguarding oneself from such a narcissist is to sever all forms of communication entirely. If the aforementioned option is not feasible, it is imperative to establish delineations and obstacles between yourselves. Prohibit any form of direct interaction or communication with them. Channel that information through a person of your confidence. The detrimental impact caused by a susceptible narcissist on one's psychological well-being is profoundly distressing, and their relentless pursuit of dominance remains ceaseless. They perceive everything as a competition or a contest, and their ultimate goal is triumph.

Invulnerable /Grandios/Overt

This represents the prevailing archetype of narcissists, often invoked by individuals upon hearing the term 'narcissist'. The invincible narcissist exhibits high levels of self-assurance, aloofness, and a distinct absence of compassion towards others. They prioritize power, recognition, and pleasure over all other considerations. Frequently, they harbor a perception of their superiority over others and possess an intrinsic desire to ensure that this sentiment is acknowledged by all. An impervious egotist desires authority and is indifferent to trampling upon others to advance themselves.

These individuals exemplify the conventional portrait of a narcissist: an individual characterized by immense self-assurance, detached demeanor, and a propensity for cruelty. Narcissists who are not susceptible to vulnerability shamelessly pursue power, glory, recognition, and pleasure. Frequently, they exhibit symptoms of a deity-like complex, harboring a belief in their own exceptionalism and possessing an insatiable compulsion to assert this superiority upon others. Their primary emphasis revolved around displays of authority, namely, the imposition of their dominance over others. The individual who presents it derives pleasure from exerting dominance over those in their vicinity.

They retain control due to an inherent desire for supremacy and control. This individual displays a consistent pattern of arrogant behavior, operating under the belief that they hold a higher position or possess superior qualities. They frequently pass judgment on others, holding them in disdain and treating them with condescension as though they were of a lower status or lacking in some way. He holds the belief that his judgments are infallible and asserts a need for complete domination over circumstances, thereby causing his mere existence to typically imbue a sense of oppression. When a narcissistic individual of this kind assumes authority, he renders the existence of his subordinates exceedingly challenging. In a romantic partnership, he employs it as a symbol of achievement. He typically favors individuals who serve purely as a vehicle for showcasing his dominance and fulfilling his requirements for control. This individual, characterized by narcissism, exhibits a pronounced inclination towards exploitative behavior, bordering on acts of mistreatment. He demonstrates his dominance by employing disdain towards others, leaving them feeling inferior and solidifying his status as a victor.

They are willing to go to any lengths to achieve success. Their objective is to achieve victory and assert dominance over others. They hold the belief that they possess a higher level of excellence relative to others, thereby justifying their entitlement to preferential treatment. This individual can be characterized as an arrogant individual who harbors a sense of superiority and a desire to constantly assert their dominance and superiority in all aspects.

www.ingramcontent.com/pod-product-compliance
Lightning Source LLC
Chambersburg PA
CBHW050246120526
44590CB00016B/2231